Wolf Moon

Poems

Red Shuttleworth

Blue Horse Press Redondo Beach, California 2020

WOLF MOON

RED SHUTTLEWORTH

Blue Horse Press
Redondo Beach
California

Copyright © 2020 Red Shuttleworth
Photographs Copyright © Jeffrey Alfier
All rights reserved.
Printed in the United States of America.

Cover art: "Vacant House on a Rural Highway"
Blue Horse Press Archives 2018

Editors: Jeffrey and Tobi Alfier
Blue Horse Press logo (1996): Amy Lynn Alfier

ISBN 978-0-578-65484-3

No part of this book may be reproduced or transmitted in any form or by any means, electronic or mechanical, including photocopy, recording, or any information storage and retrieval system now known or to be invented, without permission in writing from the publisher, except by a reviewer who wishes to quote brief passages in connection with a review written for inclusion in a magazine, newspaper or broadcast.

The moral rights of the author have been asserted.

FIRST EDITION © 2020

This and other Blue Horse Press titles may be found at www.bluehorsepress.com

Acknowledgments:

I am grateful to daughter Ciara Shuttleworth for curating this collection of poems.

Except for the author photograph, by Steve Rimple, all photographs are by Jeff Alfier.

Special thanks to Jeff and Tobi Alfier and Blue Horse Press.

For

Western Writers

**Will Bagley
and
Johnny D. Boggs**

Contents

Transit of Mercury	1
Lazarus of Spokane	2
A Bump in the Road?	3
Photo: Shop Street, Galway, Ireland	4
December…Winter	5
A Midnight Past Christmas	6
Photo: Reb's Café, Benson, Arizona	7
The Wolf Moon That Is	8
Photo: Tonopah Winter	9
Whittling Away of…	10
Sagebrush…Freezing November Fog	11
The Trouble of Clean Regret	12
Photo: Strippers on Break, Oklahoma City	13
Raspy…Cheap Cologne	14
Photo: Cochise County, Arizona	15
Spasm of Awareness	16
Trespasser on the Beyond	17
L. Freud	18
A Poem with a Confederate Flag in It	19
Colby, Kansas…Motel and Flat-Screen	20
Photo: Winnemucca, Nevada	21
No Margin for Error	22
Accrued Interest Charges	23
In the Hills Northwest of Winside, Nebraska	24
Say What You Will	25
Basalt Country…Failing Heart Valve	26
Incidental Music	27
Curve 'n Clatter of Wind	28
At 2:45 A.M.	29
Dia De Los Muertos	30
Coyotes in the Dark	31
Photo: Mt. Lemmon, Arizona	32
Soap Lake Extempore	33
Lump Sum	34
Photo: Tonopah Packard	35
Computer-Written Novella	36

Photo: Fairbank Ghost Town. Angelita b. 1918 d.1919	37
To Be Completely Honest With You	38
New Black Hole Spotted	39
Verge	40
Routine Chores and Phone Fever	41
Photo: Oxnard Underpass	42
S. Freud	43
Muck…Churchyard Tombstones	44
Oranges on a Table	45
Photo: Sonoma County Farm	46
Desert Chill	47
About the Author	49

And there were voices…

Revelations 16:18

Transit of Mercury

Tainted Buddha… a grain of black rice across the sun. The lungs are the true windows to the soul. Ghost gods at bedside, arterial blood and rhinestones: all the well-thrown marriage roses become questions.

Lazarus of Spokane

Restored after a dozen days dead… and the sky was gray
water: *Jesus wept.* There are bank robberies you cannot walk
away from. Tender cure: the nurse came and held my hand.
I could scarce open my eyes. Slant of heartbeat. Rustle
of one lung. Wakeless then like a black moon crater,
I carried pocketfuls of small stones across the Jornada
del Muerto. Verily, I never left blood-clotted Spokane.

Jesus wept. Thus reliquaries and monks with hemp ropes
for waist belts. So it was that I took wine and bread-lump.
Restored after a dozen days dead, I woke with guilt-fear,
softly asked my girlfriend, *Where'd you find the car?*

Blackening night. Stacked gravestones for sale.
After the robbery… the Pontiac fishtailing on a mud
road… motor gunned to leave Ojibwa, Wisconsin….
Sack of money lost. Yet… yes, Jesus fucking wept.
Angels in translucent cotton. Is that possible?
Memory is passage from one dimension to another?
There are stones made from blood, for Lazarus lives.

A Bump in the Road?

Light rain. Memory of a madwoman and stone stairs... the reading of tea leaves: *Watch for an eagle perched at the top of a leafy poplar.* Today, decades later: the eagle. My grown children leave ikons to me.

Shop Street, Galway, Ireland

December... Winter

Ice in the shade of non-native pines... the maple. Venus naps, the sun spins toward.... The sky is a stranger we wish to love. A few days later... or days before: an icy-stone shadow crosses our dead nocturnal moon.

A Midnight Past Christmas

Absence of wind from the north, a sky speckled with stars.
Later: frost on coyote fur. I am playing with a rail spike
dagger… with a twist-handle painted blood-red.

Here we go: an old girlfriend finds me on Facebook…
fifty years after the fact. Kathy was a break-thermometer
beauty… with presents for my friends' children.

At one age or another, you might reckon there is no
key to anything. You either luck-out or get stomped
by the Devil's hooves. In a decade of leather dice cups,

Powers Irish Whiskey, sheets of coastal rain, I sliced
apples with a Bowie. Later, closer than half a decade, it was
tequila with bank-robbin' twin brothers, *Love that chicken gravy.*

Reb's Café, Benson, Arizona

The Wolf Moon That Is

The aged may feel left behind… or hatched in
a grotesque time. Voluntarily buttoned to the neck,
ghosts blotch the snowy darkness. Past midnight.
January like crumbly Irish rose petals in a poetry
collection by Thomas MacDonagh. Past midnight.

Feeling southed in a large room, almost an atrium….
No fucking let-up, a voice comes to you from inside
your shock-wavering skull. *Thought is companion.*

Wet snow at the front door, dark cattle further on,
a dwarfish pony somewhere behind the house.
Past midnight. Soak your fist in brine. Go another
round. The score goes in circles, without win or loss
past midnight. Cheap cigar, moon-bright bourbon.

Tonopah Winter

Whittling Away of….

Once a year a parched-dog tall glass… whiskey ditch. I could be extinct. Flaws 'n failures. Great Plains snow like curdled cream… in memory. So they sawed through a rib or two for the lobectomy.

Sagebrush... Freezing November Fog

On the thirteenth day of dying, a daughter gave me a fauxhawk. Little-known facts on the American West.... Wyatt Earp's wives were all self-cutters. Ice pearls 'n blood.

The Trouble of Clean Regret

Back at the end, before you start over again, you remember
her long rain-drenched hair… pastel flowers and leaves…
October like cans of chicken noodle soup and Saltines.

Or there is no starting over… an old house with dirty
windows, bug-eyed ranch children never dreaming
they'll want to break away, head for stark suburbia…

and you know she'll never lose her shine or take
to pills or store-front alternative medicine gurus.
Back at the end, you take turns speaking from slender books.

Strippers on Break, Oklahoma City

Raspy... Cheap Cologne

Copper daylight fades. Barns... brave horses... leather-thin saddles creaking from rafter chains. Record high temp... near 50. We used to make fire on corn stubble, signals to any Gaelic goddess.

Cochise County, Arizona

Spasm of Awareness

At the Spokane Death House, we had bland vegan pizza
before I saw the cardiologist. It had been months
since I had been dead some fifteen days on the sixth floor.
No one remembers precise details about carcasses.
Best to be forgotten. After the cafeteria brunch,
I sat the chapel as if it was a narcoticized horse.
As if I had cracked open my coffin for a stroll.
The chaplain came in with soda bread and wine.
A grizzly bear sang County Derry ballads
at my memorial. Now and Then get conflated.
Yellow wildflowers. Haunch of Hereford.
My death-gape face in a mirror, no breath.
Okay, so sometimes it is better to slash memory.

Trespasser on the Beyond

What there was of sky was burning black.

Valley twilight. Turtle-green tents. A sour breeze.
The rattlesnake bitten hobbled to the factory.

Sorrow carries no answers.

The Vegas pancake house had a bright turquoise carpet.
Off-work hookers… loose denim cut-offs and red lace tops.

We drank bottled beer and stared at the changing departure sign.

My howl-tangle postcards to Joseph Beuys were eventually
returned. His estate had no coyotes for a dispersal sale.

We'd just started writing. We claimed to be the *avant-garde*.

Black mashed potatoes with real butter. Bison bone buttons.
The children played ring-around-the-rosary under a black sky.

You don't necessarily *feel* dead. And there is dreaming.

Then Peter opened his mouth and said, "It's true: I perceive
that God is no respecter of persons." A lot were in disbelief.

Shame, the residue of sorrow, is also without answers.

L. Freud

Another dead-bone late night. As he paints a green-dappled
fat woman, he near believes he has returned to his boy-self…
his eyes at ease with any feast… trout or muscle churn
and moist kiss of fashion model. Steady eye… no gape,
he paints with stubby hog-hair brushes… each moment a tale.

You love my behind, don't you, my dear, Henrietta smiles.
And she transports him back to the age of horse-drawn London.
A bowl of blueberries is brought in, set on a paint-spotted table.
A small greyhound yawns at the naked woman on a bed.
Henrietta smiles, tender thrust of leg, *If only we had black wings.*

Taking a half-moment for himself, he looks out a window
as freezing rain falls softly on silver ice. Hours to breakfast.
Revived, he adds a smudge of purple to a breast, an ember-
yellow look on the loose belly, speaks of Francis Bacon's
freedoms… looseness of hand… *Freedom… yes… like ancient*

yellow scrolls becoming powder… dried egg yolk… a love-howl.

A Poem with a Confederate Flag in It

Green and sparkle-blue roofs in the distance... suburbs
jammed with escapees from rusted-out airplane wings.
Lawns of green flesh. Then a next town like the one
before even the one before that one. No home supper
table tonight. I am driving south of Lexington
toward the Little Blue River. The steel rails are dead
in Fairbury, Nebraska. I'm driving southward,

listening to Don Williams, "Good Ole Boys Like Me."
The car steers me away from the Little Blue, over
into Willa Cather's town. I'm not in a rush. My death
was converted into a reprieve, but I don't know it yet.
I am driving delirium, listening to Waylon sing
a Jim Casey song about a dying country singer,
about a Sioux Falls concert, *We all come to see him.*

Blue jeans, dial rotary phones, red Oklahoma dirt,
downtown-brick empty store fronts, finally a cafe
with a waitress name of Piper who's got a raven
tattooed over her heart. It's dark now outside.
The wind sends soda cans rattling across a motel
parking lot. This town has been gouged away
from the AAA guidebook. Motel clerk shabby-

grimaces at me, shrugs at my C-card, gives me
a room stale with cigarette smoke from a Hank song.

Colby, Kansas... Motel and Flat-Screen

Someone left a note for the maid... squiggly
handwriting on Gampi. Drear-white walls...

sheet-stink of cigar. The nearby cafe

is for drunks, for those scratching backwards
and looking up at a bad print of the canals of Venice.

Sunrise is like some sort of fetishy postcard thing.

*Dear Motel Maid, I ain't been asking favors, no,
only that you chase off them skateboarders*

'fore I shoot them deader 'n yer grandparents.

A fugitive kind of girl in a kerchief and ankle-
long splatter-blue dress... and she's loading

lost-on-the-road broken bales of Dakota hay.

Winnemucca, Nevada

No Margin for Error

The land line is dead again. Boots are too tight to go six
feet down. Snake fang. Cheap-money bus window: follow
the smoke to torn 'n crumpled Bibles. You bruised or haunted?

Accrued Interest Charges

The farm. The grace of creeks in summer.
Dry creek beds in winter for coyote escape.

Quarrel-tongue stench. Grip 'n rip a homer.
I stared at the 377 sign my fly ball failed to reach.

Rosanne Cash and Steve Earle singing,
I'll Change for You. Breezy stare of a pretty girl.

Call me at that stone hotel… the old one with
seashells in the lobby fountain… the Vertigo Inn.

Self-confidence. Opal 'n silver jewelry. We are
nearing exactly what we paid so dearly for.

In the Hills Northwest of Winside, Nebraska

Time gets sacked in the passage of horseback hours.
Loose threads, blood and viscera, ancient crumbly
letters and diaries of lonesome farm widow women:
a canteen of Kessler's and water revives... gives spirit.

It is summer of a caked-blood otherness-time:
Frank and Jesse, on stolen blind draft horses,
ride slow toward me, doff sweat-filth horse trader
hats with dry blood-spatter spots. They are thin,

like, *Who put clothes on them yard rakes?*
Jesse grins-cold, one leg shot up in Northville.
Frank nods, offers Isaiah 13:11, *I will punish
the world for their evil... and the wicked for....*

Around us are federal set-aside acres once in
fence-row to fence-row corn... new grass, not quite
native grass, is up and wary of buffalo to the roots.
I pass my whiskey canteen to Jesse who lifts it grim.

Frank asks, *Ever seen a fire that bleeds artery blood, seen
a people of blue skin from the hills of Kentucky?* He shrugs,
notes the End Times are at hand, *No one's gonna
believe, but you ought shake hands of the James Boys.*

Say What You Will

Grass-fed meat, Black Angus… grave panting in the stock trailer. Maybe you're on the downside of Colorado blondes. Trims of dawn sunlight, forty-minute funerals, bloodshed is always about *something else*.

Basalt Country... Failing Heart Valve

Soggy ground between cliffs... a rainy, warm January...
coyotes with chills... fever. I take the black leather medicine
pouch from the saddlebag: a Nevada City Winery cork,
a Stinson Beach shell, a cutting of black and gray hair
from a Wolfhound dead some years, grizzly molar,
silver Irish coins with a harp, and, most useless...
a Canadian penny. An old Derry Druidess kept
for herself wet tea leaves, half-offered her daughter.
Three counts before false moon... wolf hour... time for
the blood pressure to tank... drop way too low
for life. My gloved fists slow 'n ache as they strike.
The downstairs heavy bag barely swings
off a support beam... no Sonny Liston thuds
to James Brown's *Night Train*. Wreck 'n snap...

Incidental Music

Fluffy laundry on one town's clotheslines, a skinny
scream of an August breeze, and then I was ten miles
out into cow country, heading north for dark, thick clouds.

It was a time of local radio… every fifty miles Merle giving
way to John Denver and then it was Charlie Pride.
I sang along… saucy rodeo queens in delicate

smoky-blue thongs, rank horses, six-shooter fugitives.
It was gas station-garages, split retread tires, Cope spit,
a Nebraska barmaid… red nails, lacquered blonde hair.

Evening on the road: small scoop of mashed potatoes,
stiff slice of dry pork, side of chunky apple sauce.
Cashier, paunched and bald, nodded a daffy grin.

Curve 'n Clatter of Wind

Churchyard sand, dry brush… Jesus gone elsewhere
for whatever prize. It's like cloud-debris after a tornado.

Join the Wine Club, get midnight deliveries. It's the waiting
that makes for craziness. And drunken slobber-wet smiles.

The Devil has to try harder these days, offer downcast eyes
of innocence and piety. Zero is a grumpy number to deny.

Maybe all the cinder block motels of Garden City are gone.
Maybe. Maybe the town is a soup bone of its yesterdays.

You want to cut north for Nebraska on this haunted drive,
keep stony track of Sepsis fever, find a bank to take down.

At 2:45 A.M.

Sting of ankle skin. Something like dripping tap water
in a photo studio. Out of bed I walk through a dream-
restaurant, waiters serving lamb chops topped
with mint jelly. No coyotes at the feast.

Honey, take off your blouse, sometimes failed
to pause one of our arguments. It was mumble-dark
night. Iron gates elsewhere in front of blood-soil.
I dialed a phone, got a can of mango juice sent to me.

Scent of Irish soda bread being baked. Gibberish
of racetrack touts, *Bet the hound name a Velvet Kiss*.
Winter desert. A spider-bit ankle....

Enormous ravens and diamond-layered crones....
The brain is poorly cushioned against being
rocked by punches. Nightmares... *cobblestones*.

Dia De Los Muertos

Rest easy on a train… before you are stranded and gut-bleeding, vomit-soaked. *After takin' down a bank,* Ned said to Rupe 'n me, *you can sleep like a child.* I'm farther now from those voices.

Coyotes in the Dark

The doctor did a fancy back-kick to close the door, *You still drink? Might as well at this dice roll.* The black lace night, coyotes and maybe a sick calf: snow and blood by morning. Flashlight beam… barren field.

Mount Lemmon, Arizona

Soap Lake Extempore

Vape pipe... meth pipe. Sunshine rises with venereal yeasty
drip. Gas station coffee for cops, silver duct tape for bat-
hammered side windows, 'n it's take-to-bed for the midnight
package delivery boys. Sweet leafy light up Road 20... orchards
with windfall apples... a mange-skinny coyote pack eats quick.

March will come... sure as federal high ground cyanide traps.
Then a vinyl Easter, no CD's, for the folks living gibberish
tirades in big houses... golf course and ball-shattered windows.
All year long, bottled water, whipped cream-full cannisters

huffed-empty, tossed in ditches north to the coulees.
I wanna have an awake mind, the prom queen gas clerk says,
applies blackberry lipstick to her top lip, vanilla-peach
to the lower one. Used car lot... a salesman coughs,
says, *I wanna work with you* to a fired topless dancer.

Lump Sum

That winter windshields froze because our one gas
station used dirty windshield water instead of washer-

blue fluid. Drivers staggered out of wrecked, ditched cars...
beefy men and narrow-shouldered city cousins in for Christmas.

Years later, on her thick wool cloak from Donegal, to the shuffle
of hobbled rental horses, a lack of prayer.... Roses blossom on stone?

There are so many B-movies, characters in fake-distress.
I was working a push mower on cheat grass, young sage, balding

plain old lawn grass.... A plume of smoke rose from a far-
neighbor's pasture, a grayish-green cloud... someone's yesterdays.

Tonopah Packard

Computer-Written Novella

She had slight shoulders. She made him herbal tea. He was chalky. Already cremated, spread on a gravel two-track, he was truly addled. She kept going to work, laundering bridegroom bedsheets, crying doom.

Fairbank Ghost Town. Angelita, b. 1918, d. 1919

To Be Completely Honest with You

Deception is a meteor… a rustle of light… a lap around the cosmos. The game is mosquito-light. A light heavyweight's left hook led to seeing clouds. She ordered Canadian bacon. Love and guitar-prayer.

New Black Hole Spotted

A wide pasture-burn and lots of smoke. It is Easter. Bunnies and rebellion. The first to throw mud gets a candy-colored plastic radio. Champagne. Then porch blood to hose away.

Verge

Discard the whiskey bottles… not exactly trophies of birth or win. Some ride dead horses. Some swim concrete of empty swim pools. The heart falls apart, stent 'n new valve. Jaw of an open clay grave.

Routine Chores and Phone Fever

A new decade begins with straw bales and a spark. A slack
brain, a vast field of corn stubble with blue cattle, boxes of mouse
poison to distribute between mushy walls: an old friend spills
a vodka and soda, phones from a city's half-darkened sky.

I can only wrong-imagine penthouse life, a butler serving
oily sardines and Ritz crackers, soot-gray windows....
If I was still dipping Copenhagen, spitting into soda cans, pouring
three-fingers cheap bourbon to take long distance memories.

A rare January south wind is rustling modest high desert pines.
Curiosity about Asiatic shamans... chicken-bone readers.
What persists to the coffin: cattle at barb wire, salt 'n mineral
blocks tossed from the back of a pickup, a frothy-white moon.

Oxnard Underpass

S. Freud

For some it begins with ritual, constant washing of hands...
grabbing one clean white shirt after another... and the tough
train for failure... lapses... glasses that must be sponged clean
two or three times before one adds fruit juicy punch.

The train leaves the depot in Fairbury, the last train ever,
rolls 'n jerks for Wyoming. A needle scratches across a record.
Spade Cooley is singing in his best regret-murder voice.

Tremble and snort... lines of white coke. Dream of Gravesend.
The jaw-pain is tolerable. Freud, fist within a blue silk stocking....

Muck… Churchyard Tombstones

Comic books with ads for toenail fungus remedies, high Gaelic stone crosses, a woman baking a box of apples: the ocean volunteered up the cliff. Naked 'n pale, she dried her great grandmother's funeral cloak.

Oranges on a Table

Stacked… empty wood apple boxes… and a tractor in the distance.
The scent of roast beef sandwiches. Hope collapses in such hours.
Loco hombre and a Colt revolver. A long silence is finally drained.

Sonoma County Farm

Desert Chill

I polish an epitaph.
Our lives are a rescue, but she never explained.

It's taken me seventy-five years to half-
believe I have a handle on my life.

Blue silk. Redwood gazebo. Black horse.
The casino suite was ankle-deep in wildflowers.

With one notebook after another since '67,
lines and notes from Kessler's or Copenhagen.

Excess is that girl purifying your absence
with a Cowboy Junkies song… on repeat.

Red Shuttleworth is a three-time recipient of Western Writers of America's Spur Award for Poetry. His *Woe to the Land Shadowing* (Blue Horse Press) won the 2016 Western Heritage Award for Best Poetry Book. In 2007, *True West* magazine named him "Best Living Western Poet." He received a 2017 Tanne Foundation Award for Poetry and Playwriting. Shuttleworth's plays have appeared widely, most recently his *Eight Monologues from Americana West*, directed by Kirk Ellis, premiered in June of 2019 in Old Tucson as part of the Western Writers of America convention.

Other works by Red Shuttleworth

Eight Monologues from Americana West

Tumbledown

Homeward

Rumors and Borders: Eight Western Plays

Straight Ahead

Woe to the Land Shadowing

High Plains Fandango

Ghosts & Birthdays

Johnny Ringo

We Drove All Night

Roadside Attractions

Western Settings

www.ingramcontent.com/pod-product-compliance
Lightning Source LLC
Chambersburg PA
CBHW041528090426
42736CB00036B/230